Winter Holidays Around the World

This book belongs to:

Westie + Winslow

Winter Holidays Around the World

Countries to Explore:

Australia
Germany
India
Sweden
Mexico
Italy
Russia
China
United Kingdom
United States
France
Israel

Table of Contents

Holidays Included in this Book

Diwali   Falls between mid-October and mid-November

Hanukkah   Starting on the 25th day of Kislev according to the Hebrew calendar, which may occur at any time from late November to late December

St. Nicholas Day   December 6th

St. Lucia Day   December 13th

Los Posadas   December 16th and ending December 24th

Winter Solstice   December 21st

Christmas   December 25th

Kwanzaa   December 26th - January 1st

New Year's Eve   December 31st

New Year's Day   January 1st

Epiphany   January 6th

Chinese New Year   The first day of the New Year falls on the new moon between January 21st and February 20th.

How to Use This Book

This unit study was designed to be used with a variety of ages, so your entire family can enjoy learning about many different countries, cultures and traditions during the holiday season. The workbook pages were designed for kids in about the 3rd to 5th grades, but this can be easily adapted for younger and older students.

For Younger Children: Pair this study with picture books from around the world (a supplemental book list can be found at www.BookandBee.com/HolidayBook) and use the questions as a starting point for family discussions.

For Older Children: Use this study as a jumping off point, and encourage them to learn more about each country and culture by conducting their own research online. My oldest made travel brochures for each country last year. This year, he is planning on creating short videos for each country as we learn about them. Encourage them to dig deeper into the topics in this book!

In order to fully enjoy this book, you'll want to make sure you have a good children's atlas on hand, or Internet access, so your kids can look up information about the countries, see the flags, and answer the questions.

Scheduling this book is simple - there are 12 countries listed, so if you do one a week, you can start in early November and use this study through the end of January. If you do two countries per week (which my family does), you can start the week before Thanksgiving, and end in mid-January.

For one country a week, you would do one to two pages a day, which would look something like this:

Day 1 : All About _____ page
Day 2: The Holiday worksheet page
Day 3: Worksheet page/Coloring
Day 4: Worksheet page/Coloring
Day 5: Hands-On Craft or Recipe

For two countries a week, you would do three to four pages a day and it would look something like this:

Day 1: All About country 1, the holiday worksheet, one additional worksheet
Day 2: Remaining worksheet pages, hands-on Craft/Recipe
Day 3: All About country 2, the holiday worksheet, one additional worksheet
Day 4: Remaining worksheet pages, hands-on Craft/Recipe
Day 5: Catch up on remaining worksheets/activities

Or, you can just hand your kids this book, and tell them to have fun with it! Don't stress about how to get it done, just jump right in and enjoy the unit study!

All About AUSTRALIA

Color the Austra-
lian flag red, white
and blue.

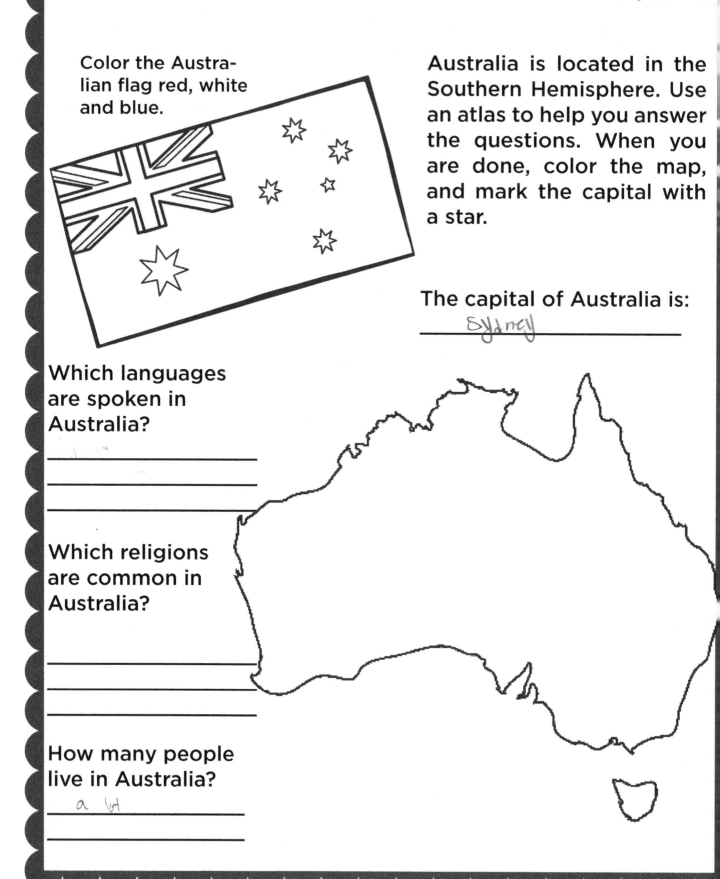

Australia is located in the
Southern Hemisphere. Use
an atlas to help you answer
the questions. When you
are done, color the map,
and mark the capital with
a star.

The capital of Australia is:

_____Sydney_____

Which languages
are spoken in
Australia?

_____
_____
_____

Which religions
are common in
Australia?

_____
_____
_____

How many people
live in Australia?

_____a lot_____
_____

Christmas in Australia

Warm Weather Traditions

Christmas in Australia is a lot like Christmas in the United States, only with one big difference-the weather! Because Australia is in the Southern Hemisphere, Christmas comes at the start of summer. The weather is warm, which means many families spend their Christmas outdoors at the park or at the beach. Some families enjoy a typical Christmas dinner of ham or turkey, but many Australian families also enjoy seafood (like lobster or shrimp) or have a big BBQ for dinner. Christmastime is also the end of the school year for Australian kids; the start of summer vacation makes the Christmas season that much more jolly!

One popular tradition in Australia is to sing "carols by candlelight." Communities come together outdoors to sit on picnic blankets and sing carols while holding candles.

Make up titles of Christmas carols you could sing during the summer (use your imagination!):

_____
_____
_____
_____
_____
_____
_____
_____

How Is It Summer There and Winter Here?

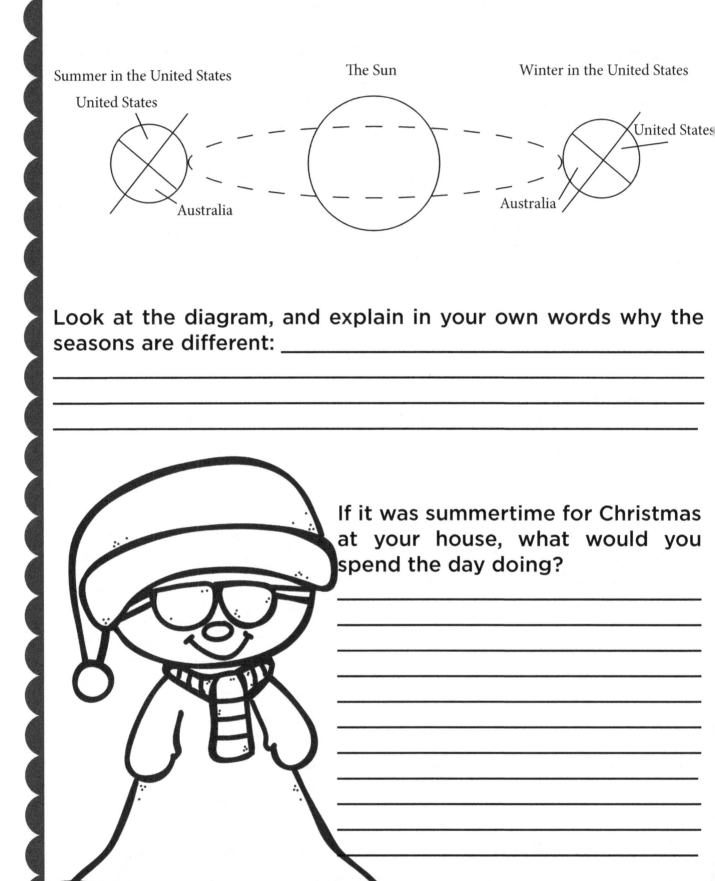

Summer in the United States

United States

Australia

The Sun

Winter in the United States

United States

Australia

Look at the diagram, and explain in your own words why the seasons are different: _____
_____
_____
_____

If it was summertime for Christmas at your house, what would you spend the day doing?

_____
_____
_____
_____
_____
_____
_____
_____
_____

Make Baked Campfire Apples

Ingredients:
Apples
3 tablespoons butter
6 tablespoons brown sugar
1 teaspoon cinnamon
Raisins
Walnuts

Directions:
1. Cut out the middle of the apple, leaving the bottom of the apple intact (like a bowl).

2. Mix the butter, sugar, cinnamon, raisins and walnuts, and then use a spoon to fill the apples with the mixture.

3. Wrap apples in tin foil, then place on coals, or on BBQ for 25 minutes. If you'd like to cook these in the oven, you can cook them at 350 degrees for 25-30 minutes.

Australian Animals

Use the word bank to fill in the blanks:

marsupials, pouch, nocturnal, deforestation, strong, jump,
balance, tallest, herds, threatened, habitat

Koalas and kangaroos are _____, which means their babies are born immature, and grow inside their mother's _____.

Koalas are often called "koala bears" but they are not bears at all. Koalas are _____, which means they are awake at night. They can sleep for more than 18-20 hours a day, so they often are asleep at night too! Many koalas are losing their homes to _____ in Australia. It is estimated that more than 80% of their habitat is gone.

Kangaroos have very _____ legs, and can _____ about 30 feet and move about 30 miles per hour! They use their strong tails for _____ and are the _____ of all the marsupials.

Kangaroos live in large groups called _____, and will stop and fight to defend their homes if they are _____. Like koalas, kangaroos are struggling with the loss of their natural _____ in Australia.

All About GERMANY

Color the German flag black, red and yellow.

Germany is a country located in Europe. Use an atlas to help you answer the questions. When you are done, color the map, and mark the capital with a star.

The capital of Germany is:

_____

Which languages are spoken in Germany?

_____
_____
_____

Which religions are common in Germany?

_____
_____
_____

How many people live in Germany?

_____
_____

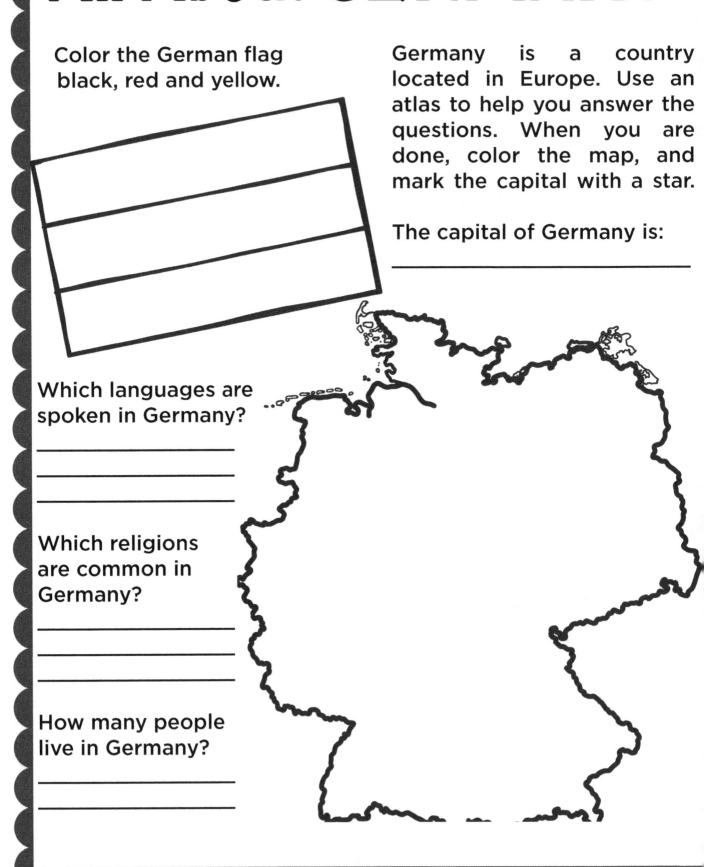

Saint Nicholas Day

A German Christmas Tradition

Saint Nicholas Day is celebrated on December 6th. On the night before, German children clean their shoes, and then leave them by the door or window overnight. If they were good, Saint Nicholas will fill them with small gifts, treats and coins, but if they were naughty, he will fill them with sticks. In some areas of the country, Saint Nicholas, who looks like a bishop and carries a staff, will go door to door visiting homes and bringing small gifts for the children. On the 6th, families enjoy the feast of Saint Nicholas and share a special meal.

In some parts of Germany, children receive gifts on December 24th. Their parents will hide the Christmas tree in the living room until the very last moment when they surprise the children with a beautifully decorated tree.

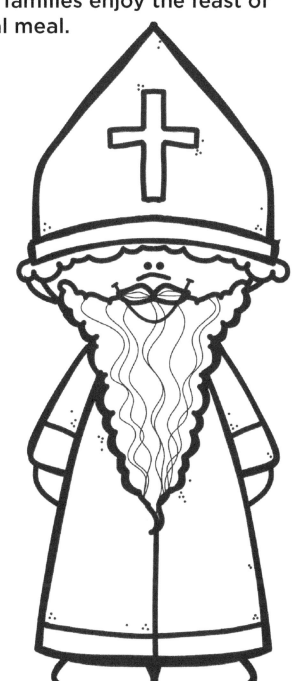

Gifts are brought by the ChristKindl, an angel-like Christ child. They open the gifts right then, on Christmas Eve.

Why do you think there are two different Christmas traditions in Germany?

_____
_____
_____
_____
_____

```
M D X H N O T L U N S N H S Q
V J J J E X K I N D E R G G Z
N Y O W T M N R X X T N E U R
W W U D H E M H V R B R C E V
V D X J C R C A E Y M S K T A
X K A B A R Y E J A A C E Z F
L N I Y N Y O J N M A A H L N
E E G L H J P Y T N S P W D E
N H O V I X N S K L D F N G T
F C O H E U I S M L Z W A T U
K S D U W R S I I L F T F X G
I E U N H U X H M Z P R P G Z
N G R C N R C G I F T O O I Q
T D M U A B T S I R H C U H N
M Y W F N U T C R A C K E R E
```

Word Search Word List:
Merry Christmas, Good Day, Child, Tree, Gift, Nutcracker, Germany, Frohe Weihnachten, Guten Tag, Kinder, Christbaum, Geschenk, Nussknacker

Fun with the German Language

Can you and your family figure out the translation of these German words?

1. Frohe Weihnachten ☐☐☐☐☐ ☐☐☐☐☐☐☐☐☐

2. Guten Tag ☐☐☐☐ ☐☐☐

3. Kinder ☐☐☐☐☐

4. Christbaum ☐☐☐☐☐☐☐☐☐ ☐☐☐☐

5. Geschenk ☐☐☐☐

6. Nussknacker ☐☐☐☐☐☐☐☐☐☐

Make German Lebkuchen

INGREDIENTS:

For the Cookies:
3 cups all-purpose flour, plus extra for kneading
1 1/4 teaspoon ground nutmeg
1 1/4 teaspoon ground cinnamon
1/2 teaspoon ground cloves
1/2 teaspoon ground allspice
1 egg
3/4 cup light brown sugar
1/2 cup honey
1/2 cup molasses

For the Glaze:
1 cup confectioner's sugar
2 tablespoons water
1 tablespoon lemon juice

DIRECTIONS:
1. Preheat the oven to 350°F.
2. Mix together the flour, nutmeg, cinnamon, cloves and allspice. Set aside.
3. Beat the egg and sugar together on medium speed until light and fluffy.
4. Add in the honey and molasses until thoroughly combined.
5. On low speed, stir in the flour mixture until just combined.
6. Turn the dough out from the bowl onto a well-floured surface. Knead the dough, adding more flour as needed, until a stiff dough is formed.
7. Chill until firm, about 2 hours.
8. On a well-floured surface, roll out the dough, and then cut into circles. Bake for 10-12 minutes.
9. Once cool, mix the glaze and spread it on top of the cookies.

Advent Wreaths

Advent wreaths are common in the United States, but did you know they originated in Germany? The legend says that a man named Johann Wichern was caring for poor children in an old farmhouse over the holiday season.

The children kept asking when Christmas was, so he built them a wreath in an old wheel. Around the wheel, he placed 20 white candles and 4 red candles. He lit a candle every day so the children could count down until Christmas.

Many modern churches use Advent wreaths, and light one candle each Sunday for the four weeks prior to Christmas. On Christmas Eve, or Christmas day, they light a 5th candle.

How does your family count down to Christmas? _____
_____
_____
_____

All About INDIA

Color the Indian flag orange, blue and green.

India is a country located in Asia. Use an atlas to help you answer the questions. When you are done, color the map, and mark the capital with a star.

The capital of India is:

_____

Which languages are spoken in India?

_____
_____
_____

Which religions are common in India?

_____
_____
_____

How many people live in India?

_____
_____
_____

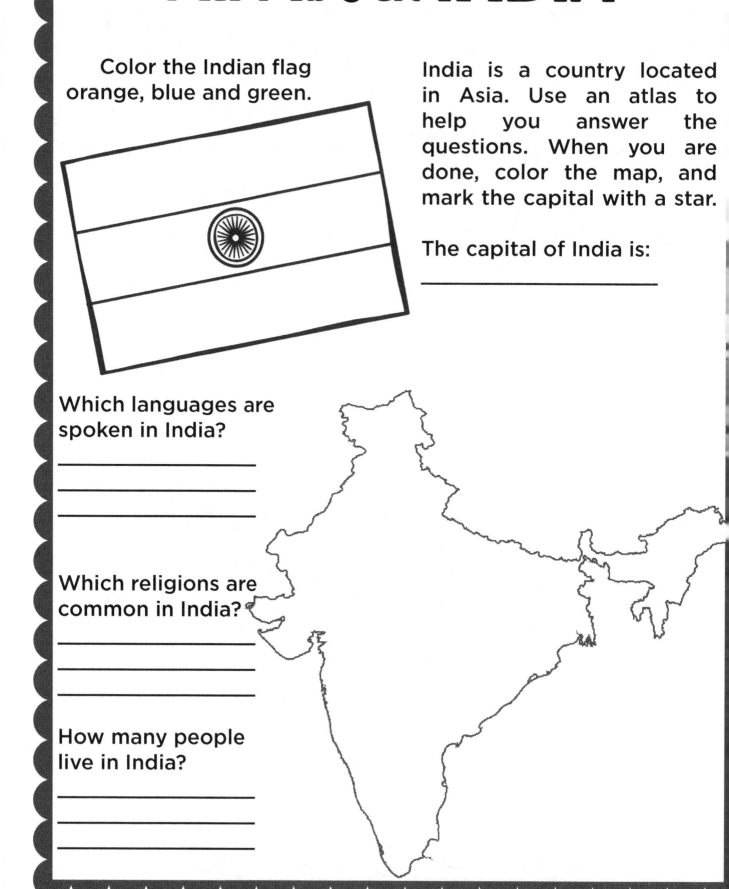

Diwali

Diwali celebrates the last harvest of the year in India. It is typically celebrated in October or November. Diwali is a national festival that is celebrated by people from many religions. Diwali lasts five days. On the first day, families clean their homes. On the second day, families decorate their homes with lamps, and make fancy designs on the ground out of colored sand. On the third day, they gather for prayer, giant feasts and fireworks. On the fourth day, they celebrate the new year by visiting friends and family and giving gifts. On the last day, brothers visit their married sisters and have a big meal together.

Getting ready for the festival is a large part of the Diwali tradition. Families clean their homes, decorate, and pick out new clothing to wear.

Why is it important to prepare for a holiday? What is your family doing to get ready for your own holiday traditions?

_____

_____

_____

_____

_____

_____

Diwali Diya

The "festival of lights" is a celebration of the victory of good over evil. Families light their special lanterns (Diya) to help the goddess Lakshmi find her way into their homes. Goddess Lakshmi is the symbol of wealth and prosperity, and families hope if she visits their home, they will have a good new year.

Color the Diwali Diya

Make Candle Holders for Diwali

Supplies:
Glass candle holders
Craft glue
Gems, sequins, beads and other decorative items (choose whatever you like!)

Directions:
1. Choose a candle holder to decorate, or create one out of craft clay.

2. With your parent's help, look online at Diwali Diyas and at other Hindu works of art.

3. Use your craft glue to create patterns and designs on your candle holder with the gems, sequins, beads - or any decorative items you like!

4. When the decorations are dry, insert a candle and enjoy your candle holder!

Fun with the Hindi Language

Can you and your family figure out the translation of these Hindi words?

1. Shush Deepavali ☐☐☐☐☐ ☐☐☐☐☐☐

2. Roshanee ☐☐ ☐☐☐

3. Namaste ☐☐☐☐☐

4. Alvida ☐☐☐☐☐☐☐

5. Aatishbaazi ☐☐☐☐☐☐☐☐☐☐

Word Search Word List:
Shush Deepavali, Roshanee, Namaste, Alvida, Aatishbaazi, Happy Diwali, light, hello, goodbye, fireworks, Lakshmi, family, home

S	L	R	N	U	V	Z	Z	J	Y	E	D
I	M	O	V	Y	A	G	L	P	Y	L	I
L	O	S	S	C	A	G	P	B	P	Z	B
A	O	H	H	O	O	A	D	N	A	F	B
V	I	A	U	W	H	O	A	A	I	C	O
A	F	N	S	Q	O	M	B	R	L	E	L
P	A	E	H	G	A	H	E	I	Q	M	L
E	M	E	T	S	S	W	L	T	W	O	E
E	I	J	T	I	O	A	S	K	X	H	H
D	L	E	T	R	W	A	L	V	I	D	A
A	Y	A	K	I	Q	L	I	G	H	T	R
P	A	S	D	I	M	H	S	K	A	L	N

All About SWEDEN

Color the Swedish flag
blue and yellow.

Sweden is a country located in Scandinavia. Use an atlas to help you answer the questions. When you are done, color the map, and mark the capital with a star.

The capital of Sweden is:

_____

Which languages are
spoken in Sweden?

_____
_____
_____

Which religions are
common in Sweden?

_____
_____
_____

How many people live in
Sweden?

_____
_____
_____

Saint Lucia Day

Saint Lucia Day is celebrated on December 13th. Lucia was a young girl who would bring food to the Christians hiding in the catacombs of Rome many years ago. She was martyred for her faith, and now people remember her by celebrating Saint Lucia Day. Each year, the oldest daughter in the family dresses in a white robe and wears a crown of candles on her head. She serves her parents buns and coffee or hot wine. People all over the country light candles in honor of the day, to celebrate goodness and light during seasons of darkness.

Why do you think Lucia wore the candles on her head instead of carrying them?

_____
_____
_____

Saint Lucia Day isn't just a family tradition; many towns choose a Lucia as well, and girls all over the country dress up in their robes and candles to visit hospitals, orphanages and old people's homes to sing to them and bring them treats.

Saint Lucia Day is about bringing light and hope to people in need. Who can you visit this holiday season?

_____
_____
_____
_____
_____

What about the boys?

Swedish boys participate in the Saint Lucia Day parades by dressing up as "Star Boys." The boys wear large paper cones on their heads and carry a paper star at the end of a stick. The cones are also decorated with stars. The Star Boys are an important part of the parade celebrating the light, and they follow Lucia and the other girls carrying candles in the parade around town.

Create Your Own
Star Boy Hat & Saint Lucia Crown

Make your own costume for Saint Lucia Day!

For Boys: **Create a cone out of a large piece of paper. Cut paper stars out of construction paper (or use star stickers) to decorate your hat.**

For Girls: **Use construction paper, or use a wreath or greenery ties from the holiday section at your local store to create a green crown. Decorate your crown with paper candles, or ask your parents to help you attach LED lights to your crown.**

Wear your costumes while delivering special Saint Lucia treats to your neighbors or to your siblings on Saint Lucia Day!

Make Lussebullar

Ingredients:
6 ounces butter, melted
2 1/2 cups lukewarm milk
3/4 teaspoon saffron
1 cup sugar
1 tablespoon instant active yeast
1/2 teaspoon salt
2 pounds wheat flour, or as needed
Beaten egg, for brushing
Raisins, for garnish

Directions:
1. Place the butter and milk in a medium bowl. Add in the yeast, sugar, salt and saffron, then let the yeast rest for 5 minutes.
2. Gradually add the flour and knead for 10 minutes. Form into a ball, and cover with a cloth.
3. Allow dough to rise for 30-45 minutes.
4. Transfer dough to a well-floured work space, and then shape into spiral shapes, braids or buns.
5. Place on baking sheet and allow to rise another 30-45 minutes.
6. Brush the buns with beaten egg, and press raisins lightly into the dough.
7. Bake at 400 degrees until golden. Smaller buns may bake for 10 minutes, and larger buns may take up to 20.
8. Cool buns on a rack before eating.

Fun with the Swedish Language

Can you and your family figure out the translation of these Swedish words?

1. Julgrann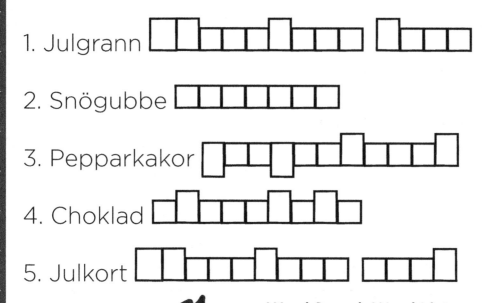

2. Snögubbe

3. Pepparkakor

4. Choklad

5. Julkort

Word Search Word List:
Julgrann, Christmas, Tree, Snogubbe, Snowman, Pepparkakor, Gingerbread, Choklad, Chocolate, Julkort, Card, Lucia, Sweden

M	B	C	H	O	K	L	A	D	F	P	G	L	W	E
I	J	R	I	D	V	K	F	Y	A	S	L	S	C	D
M	U	K	M	A	S	C	V	H	D	O	Z	A	W	S
M	L	N	C	E	K	E	H	Z	I	K	L	I	V	Y
V	K	N	A	R	Y	C	B	O	I	X	X	C	K	P
Y	O	A	R	B	M	H	N	B	C	V	M	U	A	J
P	R	R	D	R	O	R	H	P	U	O	D	L	Z	H
C	T	G	V	E	Y	I	S	F	D	G	L	R	K	M
Q	K	L	Q	G	D	S	L	W	M	G	O	A	H	Z
O	T	U	Y	N	G	T	D	M	E	B	N	N	T	P
E	T	J	Q	I	Y	M	F	P	L	D	U	Z	S	E
J	E	O	O	G	P	A	T	A	J	E	E	A	D	D
L	I	R	X	L	S	S	P	I	H	O	S	N	Z	Z
H	S	U	T	P	E	P	P	A	R	K	A	K	O	R
K	K	X	M	N	K	R	W	N	A	M	W	O	N	S

1. Christmas tree, 2. snowman, 3. gingerbread, 4. chocolate, 5. Christmas card

All About MEXICO

Color the Mexi-
can flag red, white
and green.

Mexico is a country
located in Central
America. Use an atlas
to help you answer
the questions. When
you are done, color
the map, and mark
the capital with a star.

The capital of Mexico is:

_____

Which languages are
spoken in Mexico?

_____
_____
_____

Which religions are
common in Mexico?

_____
_____
_____

How many people live in
Mexico?

_____
_____
_____

The Nine Days of Posadas

A Mexican Christmas Tradition

Los Posadas is a nine-day celebration leading up to Christmas. This festival is a reenactment of Mary and Joseph's trip to Bethlehem before Jesus's birth. The whole community comes together. Each night for the nine days, the community will pick one home where Posadas will be celebrated. The kids will dress up as Mary, Joseph, the angels, the wise men and shepherds, and go from home to home, asking to come in. All the houses will turn them away, and tell them that they do not have any room.

When the children get to the correct home, the community sings a special song together. There are two parts to the song. The people outside the home will sing the part asking for shelter and those inside the home respond by singing the part of the innkeeper who says there is no room. After a few verses are sung back and forth, the innkeeper decides to let them in. Once inside, the community celebrates with food, music, piñatas and gifts.

Everyone has an important role on Posadas - What part would you like? Why?

_____

_____

_____

_____

Word Bank: Nacimiento, Nativity, Nochebuena, Christmas Eve, Villancicos, Carols, Feliz Navidad, Muérdago, Mistletoe, Mexico

A	V	S	T	E	U	O	M	P	O	W	N	Y	Y	M
V	P	S	L	O	R	A	C	P	R	O	A	L	O	W
I	O	T	N	E	I	M	I	C	A	N	T	D	C	N
L	Q	A	C	V	C	S	L	O	B	L	I	F	I	O
L	O	Z	Z	W	S	W	Q	Y	T	V	V	T	X	A
A	G	O	H	K	R	X	J	T	S	B	I	J	E	N
N	A	O	A	T	T	I	A	Q	Q	J	T	J	M	E
C	D	K	R	S	Z	Z	X	B	O	R	Y	H	I	U
I	R	C	H	R	I	S	T	M	A	S	E	V	E	B
C	E	Z	I	K	G	F	G	U	H	U	T	C	D	E
O	U	D	A	D	I	V	A	N	Z	I	L	E	F	H
S	M	N	F	Q	A	S	C	M	Y	F	W	E	T	C
P	U	G	A	B	H	R	D	W	Y	Z	M	W	Y	O
Z	H	E	O	F	G	V	C	R	O	B	A	D	Z	N
N	G	M	I	S	T	L	E	T	O	E	T	Y	A	I

Fun with the Spanish Language

Can you and your family figure out the translation of these Spanish words?

1. Nacimiento

2. Nochebuena

3. Villancicos

4. Feliz Navidad

5. Muérdago

Make a Paper Bag Piñata

Supplies:
Paper lunch bag
Small candies or toys
Tissue paper (5 different colors)
Glue stick, stapler & scissors

Directions:
Open your paper bag and set it on the table. Fill it with candies or small toys, then staple the top closed.

Take the tissue paper and cut it into one-inch strips. Then, use your scissors to add a fringe on one side of your tissue paper strips. You'll want to cut about half way across the strip, at one-inch intervals.

Take your tissue paper fringe and start gluing it to your bag, working from the bottom to the top. Alternate colors.

Once you have decorated your bag with the tissue paper, ask your parents to help you hang the piñata! Have fun trying to whack it open with your family.

Celebrations in Mexico

Use the word bank to fill in the blanks:

blessed, nine, wise men, piñata, midnight, tamales, presents, church, Jesus, nativity

You already know that Posadas lasts _____ days in Mexico, but did you know there are many more celebrations and special days during the Christmas season?

When Posadas starts on December 16th, many people put out their nacimientos, or _____ scenes. They don't add baby _____ to the nativity scene until Nochebuena, which is Christmas Eve. On Christmas Eve, they have a big party, where they sing villancicos (Christmas carols), read from the Bible, eat tamales, and have a _____ for the kids! Christmas Day is often a quiet day for families to attend _____.
On Año Nuevo, they celebrate New Year's Eve and have a very late dinner with their family. If they are going to have a big party, it probably won't start until after _____! On January 6th, they celebrate Epiphany, which is called Día de Reyes "King's Day." They add the _____ to the nativity scene, and many children receive _____ on this day. The Christmas season is not over until February 2nd, which is Candlemas. On this day, people dress up their Niños Dios (Christ Child figures) and take them to the church to be _____. Afterward, they have a party and eat _____.

All About ITALY

Color the Italian flag red, white and green.

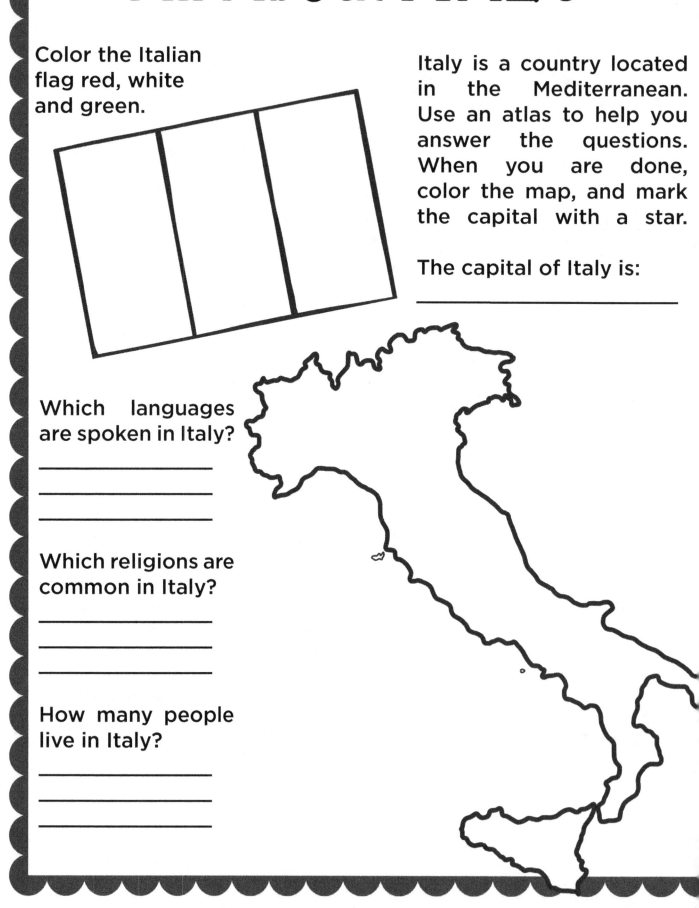

Italy is a country located in the Mediterranean. Use an atlas to help you answer the questions. When you are done, color the map, and mark the capital with a star.

The capital of Italy is:

_____

Which languages are spoken in Italy?

_____
_____
_____

Which religions are common in Italy?

_____
_____
_____

How many people live in Italy?

_____
_____
_____

La Befana

On January 6th, Italian children wake up hoping La Befana visited their homes while they were sleeping. January 6th is Epiphany, the day the three wise men visited Christ in the manger. The legend says that the three wise men stopped by Befana's home to ask for directions when they were trying to find the Christ child. They asked her to come with them on their journey, but she said no because she had too much housework to do. When they left, she regretted her decision and tried to catch up to them. She was unable to find them, but didn't know the way to the manger, so she stopped by every home along the way to give a gift to the child there in the hope that she would find the Christ child.

Why do you think Befana regretted her decision to do housework instead of help the wise men find the Christ child? What would you have done if you were her?

_____
_____
_____
_____
_____
_____
_____
_____
_____
_____
_____
_____

Help Befana Find Her Way

Use an atlas, or ask your parents to help you find where the Christ child was born. Locate Italy and mark where Befana would have started her journey to the Christ child. Draw a path from Italy to the Christ child. Then mark your home on the map.

Make Italian Torrone

Ingredients:
1 1/3 cups honey
1 cup white sugar
3 tablespoons white sugar
2 large egg whites, at room temperature
1 pinch salt
1/4 teaspoon vanilla extract
1 tablespoon lemon zest
3 cups roasted almonds
1 cup roasted pistachios

Directions:
1. Mix honey and sugar in a pot on your stove top over low heat, stirring constantly until mixture turns from grainy to silky and smooth, about 30 minutes. Remove pot from heat.
2. Place the egg whites in a mixing bowl; add a pinch of salt. Whisk until whites form soft peaks, 3 to 4 minutes. Place pot back on low heat. Gradually whisk egg white mixture in, a small amount at a time.
3. Continue cooking over low heat, stirring constantly with a spatula until mixture turns a brighter white. You'll know it's done when you mix it and a ribbon of the mixture does not immediately mix back into the rest. This will take about 40 minutes to happen.
4. Whisk in vanilla and lemon zest. Add almonds and pistachios.
5. Transfer mixture into a baking dish lined with waxed paper. Use a spatula to press the mixture down into the baking dish.
6. Allow torrone to cool completely before cutting into squares and serving.

Fun with the Italian Language

Can you and your family figure out the translation of these Italian words?

1. Babbo Natale □□□□□ □□□□□

2. Buon Natale □□□□□ □□□□□□□

3. il presepio □□□□□□□□□

4. Re Magi □□□□ □□□

5. Calza □□□□□□□

6. Gesù Bambino □□□□ □□□□□

Word Search Word List:
Babbo Natale, Santa Claus, Merry Christmas, il Presepio, Nativity, Re Magi, Wise Men, Calza, Stocking, Gesu Bambino, Baby Jesus, Italy, Befana

P	W	I	S	E	D	W	O	T	E	T	J	V	Y	Y
J	I	U	S	E	G	X	J	J	A	N	A	F	E	B
J	S	A	M	T	S	I	R	H	C	U	B	O	E	J
C	N	A	T	I	V	I	T	Y	N	A	N	N	R	I
Y	L	A	T	I	A	X	U	N	B	I	T	K	J	W
A	M	V	O	S	Z	J	F	B	B	S	V	J	R	P
L	B	E	X	T	C	V	O	M	E	U	E	B	R	J
R	F	F	N	O	L	X	A	H	M	S	A	E	C	P
B	H	Y	K	C	A	B	U	C	U	Z	S	Z	U	G
Y	H	B	M	K	U	E	M	S	L	E	E	L	L	L
O	K	A	A	I	S	L	P	A	P	E	V	F	U	O
D	R	B	G	N	J	A	C	I	K	L	X	V	U	B
G	N	B	I	G	L	T	O	Z	I	J	C	T	C	R
K	Y	X	J	F	M	A	D	U	X	Q	T	P	K	Z
S	A	N	T	A	A	N	K	M	E	R	R	Y	F	W

All About RUSSIA

Color the Russian flag
white, blue and red

Russia is a country located in Eurasia. Use an atlas to help you answer the questions. When you are done, color the map, and mark the capital with a star.

The capital of Russia is:

_____

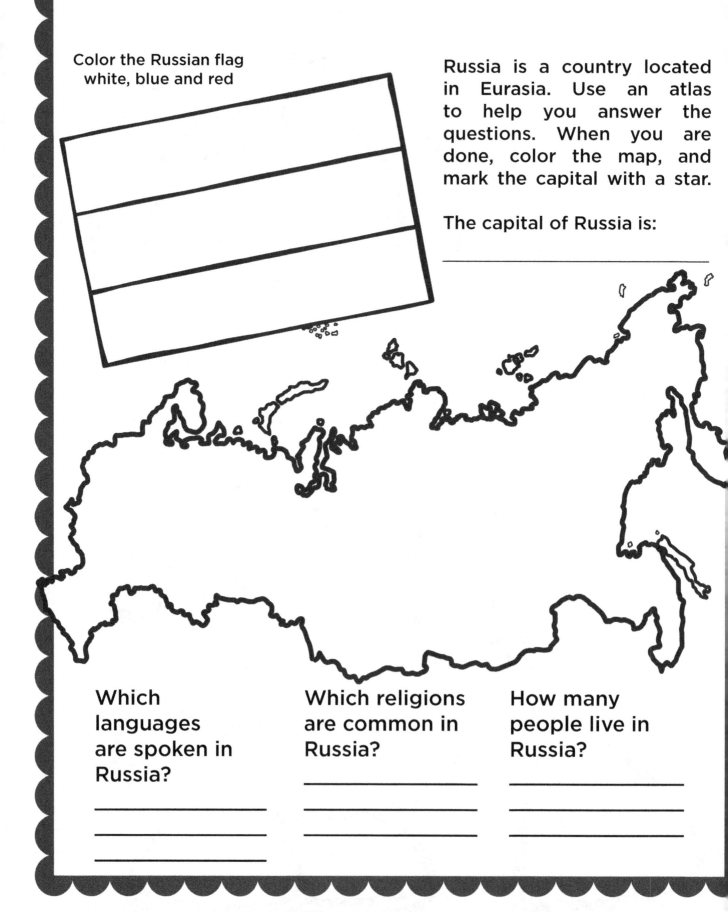

Which languages are spoken in Russia?

_____

_____

_____

Which religions are common in Russia?

_____

_____

_____

How many people live in Russia?

_____

_____

Grandfather Frost in Russia

On New Year's Day, "Grandfather Frost" (called Ded Moroz) brings presents to children in Russia. Ded Moroz always travels with his granddaughter, the Snow Maiden, Snegurochka. Ded Moroz's sleigh is pulled by three, large Russian horses, and he always carries a big, magic staff. Ded Moroz does not live at the North Pole - he lives in a Russian town called Veliky Ustyug. Russian children can visit this town to see his horses and meet Ded Moroz before New Year.

On New Year's Eve, children hold hands, make a circle around the Christmas tree, and call for Snegurochka or Ded Moroz to come. When they do this, the star and other lights on the Christmas tree light up and the children know Ded Moroz is coming!

Does your family have any special traditions for decorating or lighting the Christmas tree?

_____
_____
_____
_____
_____
_____
_____
_____
_____

Word Search Word List:
S Novym Godo, Happy New Year, Tree,
Snegurochka, Ded Moroz, Russia, Father Frost,
Troika, Sleigh, Sneg, Snow

D	L	M	K	Z	B	J	T	D	Z	W	E	N	A	A
U	E	W	Z	X	T	T	R	O	I	K	A	K	I	S
Y	W	D	J	U	T	B	R	N	W	N	H	S	B	Z
T	L	S	N	O	W	A	M	X	F	C	S	I	U	O
R	K	V	H	H	E	C	F	K	O	U	K	Y	G	R
E	W	G	A	Y	X	X	A	R	R	R	V	S	E	O
E	N	P	D	T	E	D	U	E	L	O	L	M	N	M
F	P	P	L	D	T	G	P	Z	C	E	G	F	S	E
Y	L	S	B	S	E	F	F	M	I	G	A	A	E	K
I	F	G	J	N	O	V	T	G	I	U	I	T	Q	Y
X	R	X	S	A	Q	W	H	E	N	E	N	H	D	N
E	X	O	D	O	G	M	Y	V	O	N	S	E	S	I
W	Y	O	B	T	V	W	E	U	S	G	L	R	S	C
Z	N	T	S	O	R	F	T	L	Y	W	G	B	W	M
S	F	J	A	E	R	V	O	U	Y	W	D	U	F	B

Fun with the Russian Language

Can you and your family figure out the translation of these Russian words?

1. S Novym Godo ☐☐☐☐☐ ☐☐☐ ☐☐☐☐

2. Yolka ☐☐☐ ☐☐☐☐☐ ☐☐☐☐

3. Ded Moroz ☐☐☐☐☐☐ ☐☐☐☐☐

4. Troika ☐☐☐☐☐ ☐

5. Sneg ☐☐☐☐

Make Russian Borscht

Ingredients:

Olive oil or vegetable oil
1 pound of stew beef
1 large onion
8 cups beef broth or beef stock, divided
4 large beets

4 carrots
1 large russet potato
2 cups thinly sliced cabbage
3/4 cup chopped fresh dill
3 tablespoons red wine vinegar
1 cup sour cream
Salt and Pepper

Directions:

1. Brown the beef in 2 teaspoons of oil. Add onion, cook and soften, about 5 minutes.
2. Pour 4 cups of beef broth over the beef and onions in the pot. Bring to a boil. Lower the heat to a simmer, cover and cook until the meat is falling-off-the-bone tender, about 1 hour 30 minutes.
3. While the beef is cooking, peel and chop the beets, carrots, and potatoes into 1/2-inch pieces. Toss the vegetables with a teaspoon or two of olive oil and spread them out in a single layer on a foil lined roasting pan. Roast in a 400°F oven for 15 minutes.
4. Remove the meat from the pot & chop the meat into bite-sized pieces.
5. Return the pot to the stove and add the remaining broth, the carrots, beets, and the diced potato. Add the chopped meat to the pot, the sliced cabbage, and a half cup of the fresh dill. Bring to a simmer, and cook for another 15 minutes or so, until the cabbage is cooked through.
6. Add the vinegar and season to taste with salt and pepper.
7. Serve with a dollop of sour cream!

A little history. . .

Russia used to be called the Soviet Union. When it was the Soviet Union, they had many laws controlling what people were allowed to do, what religious people could believe in, and what traditions they could have. Before 1991, it was illegal to celebrate Christmas in the Soviet Union.

After the Soviet Union fell, Russians were free to celebrate Christmas. Christmas is a religious holiday and is celebrated on January 7th, when families attend church and have a special dinner together.

How would you feel if your family was told they could not celebrate an important holiday? What would your family do?

_____

_____

_____

_____

_____

_____

_____

_____

All About CHINA

Color the Chinese flag red and white.

China is a country located in Asia. Use an atlas to help you answer the questions. When you are done, color the map, and mark the capital with a star.

The capital of China is:

_____

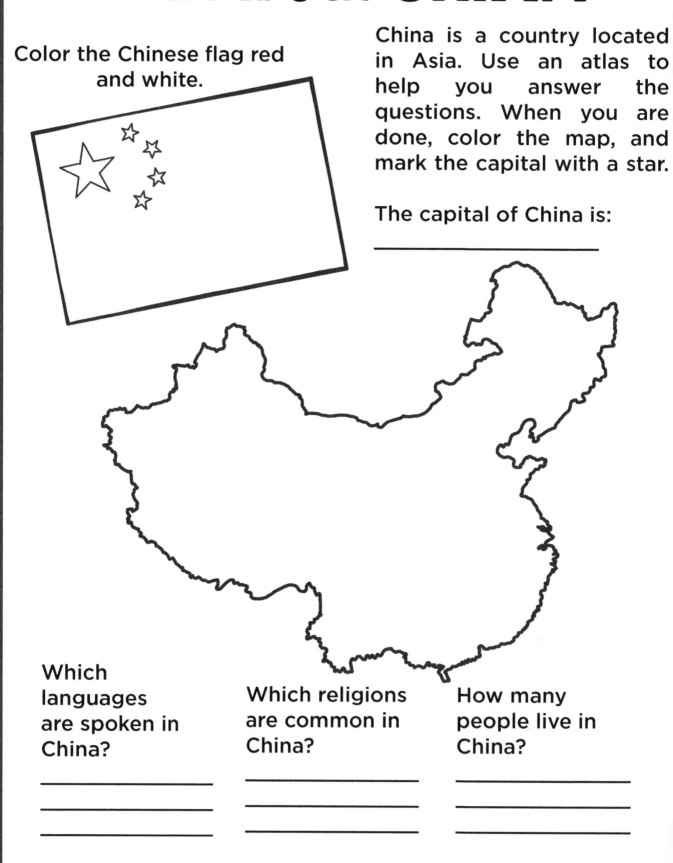

Which languages are spoken in China?

_____
_____
_____

Which religions are common in China?

_____
_____
_____

How many people live in China?

_____
_____
_____

Chinese New Year

On New Year's Eve, families travel long distances to go home to spend the day with all of their relatives. Everyone will dress in their best clothing and be on their best behavior while the head of the household makes offerings to the various gods of the house and to the family's ancestors.

Each member of the family will kneel in front of the ancestral tablets, which symbolize past generations and all of the people who came before them. Children will also kneel in respect to their elders (parents and grandparents) and if they are very

good, they'll receive a little red envelope with cash in it under their pillow on New Year.

On New Year's Day, family members will visit with each other, with their neighbors and other loved ones. They will serve "lucky" food, say "lucky" phrases and do their best to ensure the New Year will be a good and lucky year for all the people they love!

Honoring ancestors is an important part of Chinese culture. Do you know your family's history? Ask your parents or grandparents to tell you a story about one of your ancestors!

_____
_____
_____

The Lantern Festival

Use the word bank to fill in the blanks.

full, family, parades, firecrackers, houses, lantern, fill, festival, dances, lunar, beautiful, light, paper

The _____ festival happens on the 15th day of the New Year's celebrations in China. Because China follows the _____ calendar, this festival always lands on the day of the first _____ moon of the year. The night is brightly lit by the moon, and children _____ the sky with their bright _____ lanterns. Children in China make their special paper lanterns with their _____. Some communities have contests to see who can make the best and most _____ paper lantern. When it gets dark, everyone will come together and _____ their lanterns. Many towns and cities will also decorate with paper lanterns everywhere. They will be hung from _____ and businesses and in the center of town. It really is a beautiful _____ of light! During the festival, communities will also have _____ where you can see the Chinese lion and dragon _____ (ask your parents to show you a video of this on the computer!), and people light off _____ and fireworks.

Make Fortune Cookies

Ingredients:
2 large egg whites
1⁄3 cup sugar
4 tablespoons melted butter, cooled
1⁄2 cup flour
1⁄4 teaspoon salt
1⁄2 teaspoon almond extract
1⁄2 teaspoon lemon extract
Optional: 2 1/2 x 1/2-inch fortune strips

Directions:
1. Preheat oven to 350°F.
2. Grease a cookie sheet thoroughly.
3. Whip the egg whites on low speed until light and foamy.
Blend in the sugar and continue to beat until soft peaks form.
Pour in the melted butter, flour, salt, and extracts; mix until well combined.
4. Drop a tablespoon of the batter onto the prepared cookie sheet.
Using the back of a spoon, spread the batter evenly into very thin
3-inch rounds. You must work quickly to shape these cookies when
they are warm so bake just 3 at a time.
5. Bake for about 5-8 minutes or until the edges are a light golden
color.
6. Have your parents help you with this step. Quickly remove the
cookies with a spatula and place on a work surface. Lay a fortune in
the lower middle of the cookie, and fold in half to make a semi-circle.
Bend the edges up toward each other to make a crescent and pinch
ends together.
7. Cool in mini muffin tins to hold shape until crisp.
8. Repeat with remaining batter.

Fun with the Chinese Language

Calligraphy, or the art of writing, is an important art form in China. It can be difficult to learn to read and write Chinese because you cannot sound out Chinese symbols. Instead, you need to learn each word by memorizing its unique symbol. Many people do this by writing and rewriting the symbol until they have memorized it.

Try to write these Chinese symbols:

Beautiful

美

Happiness

喜

Hope

希

Wisdom

智

All About the UK

Color the Union Jack red, white and blue.

England is a country located in the United Kingdom. Use an atlas to help you answer the questions. When you are done, color the map, and mark the capital with a star.

The capital of England is:

_____

Which languages are spoken in England?

_____

_____

_____

Which religions are common in England?

_____

_____

_____

How many people live in England?

_____

_____

_____

Christmas in the UK

In the UK, most villages, towns and cities are decorated with Christmas lights during Christmas. Often a famous person switches them on. The most famous Christmas lights in the UK are on Oxford Street in London. Every year they get bigger and better. Thousands of people go to watch the big "switch on" in November at the start of the holiday season.

Children believe that Father Christmas leaves presents in stockings or pillow cases. These are normally hung up by the fire or by the children's beds on Christmas Eve. Children sometimes leave out mince pies and brandy for Father Christmas to eat and drink when he visits them. Now, some people say that a non-alcoholic drink should be left for Santa as he has to drive!

Children write letters to Father Christmas listing their requests, but sometimes instead of putting them in the post, the letters are tossed into the fireplace. The smoke carries the letters up the chimney and Father Christmas/Santa reads the smoke.

Do you write letters to Santa Claus in your family? How do the letters get to Santa?

_____
_____
_____
_____

The Queen's Christmas Message

Every year at three o'clock on Christmas Day, the Queen of England delivers a Christmas message to the people of the United Kingdom. Families all over the country gather around the TV every year to listen to her speak. During the speech, she talks about all of the wonderful things that happened in the UK that year. She always shares her thoughts on Christmas and calls on people to be kind to one another, to have hope and share the Christmas spirit. You can watch the Queen's Christmas message online if you'd like to see it this year!

Does your family have a traditional show or movie you watch every year for the holidays?

_____

_____

_____

_____

Make Sticky Toffee Pudding

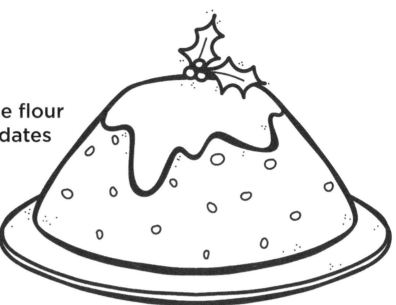

Ingredients,

Pudding,
1/4 cup (1/2 stick) butter
1 1/2 cups sifted all-purpose flour
1 1/2 cups chopped pitted dates
1 teaspoon baking soda
1 teaspoon baking powder
1/2 teaspoon sea salt
1 cup sugar
1 teaspoon vanilla extract
2 large eggs

Sauce,
1 1/4 cups (packed) light brown sugar
1/2 cup heavy cream
1/4 cup butter
1/2 teaspoon vanilla

Instructions,

1. Preheat oven to 350°F. Butter and flour Bundt pan.
2. Bring dates and 1 1/4 cups water to a boil. Remove from heat; stir in baking soda (mixture will become foamy). Set aside; let cool.
3. Whisk 1 1/2 cups flour, baking powder, and salt in a bowl.
4. Beat 1/4 cup butter, sugar, and vanilla in a large bowl to blend (mixture will be grainy). Add 2 eggs. Add flour mixture and date mixture and mix.
5. Bake 40-45 minutes. Let cool in pan on a wire rack for 30 minutes. Invert pudding onto rack.

For sauce,

1. Bring sugar, cream, and butter to a boil, stirring constantly.
2. Continue to boil, stirring constantly, for 3 minutes.
3. Remove from heat and stir in vanilla.

Cut cake into wedges. Serve with sauce and whipped cream.

Winter Solstice

The earth is tilted, and it is because of this tilt that we have seasons. When the Northern Hemisphere leans toward the sun, it's summer in the north and winter in the south. It is winter in the north when the Northern Hemisphere is tilted away from the sun.

During the winter solstice, the earth's axis is tilted at its furthest point from the sun. This means that, for us in the Northern Hemisphere, the sun is at its lowest point in the sky. Solstice is the the shortest day of the year - and the longest night. Many families around the world celebrate by coming together, burning candles or lighting fires, and celebrating the cycle of the year as days begin to grow longer following the longest night.

Label the four seasons, the Winter Solstice, and Summer Solstice on the diagram.

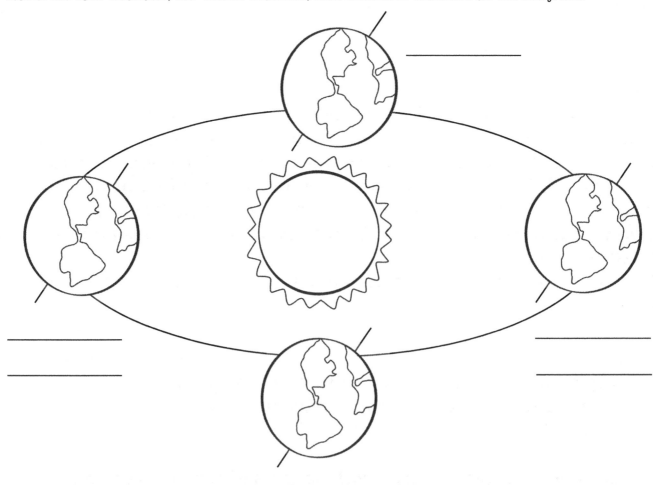

Celebrating the Longest Night at Stonehenge

Use the word bank to fill in the blanks:

winter, sunrise, 5,000, light, shorter, ancient, standing, solstice, time, Stonehenge

Stonehenge is one of the most famous _____ monuments and is made up of a ring of _____ stones which are larger than cars - about 13 feet tall! Stonehenge was built in stages, but some parts of the monument are about _____ years old.

Many ancient cultures studied the passage of _____ and focused on sunlight. Sunlight kept them warm, helped crops grow, and made it easy to see. In the winter, they may have felt fear as days became _____ and colder. It isn't suprising that they wished the light would return! The _____ solstice is the longest night of the year.

It is believed that this yearly cycle is what inspired ancient people to build _____. The stones are set in a circle and line up perfectly to the sunset of the winter solstice and the _____ of the summer solstice.

Today, many people still gather at Stonehenge to celebrate the _____ and to watch the _____ fall on the heart of the monument at the beginning of the longest night.

Fun with British Phrases

Sit down with your family and have fun guessing what these phrases and words mean!

1. That takes the biscuit!
2. A fortnight
3. And Bob's your uncle.
4. You really know your onions!
5. I really lost the plot.
6. That's smashing!
7. You're the dog's dinner tonight.
8. She's dodgy.

Write your own story using some of the words and phrases shown here:

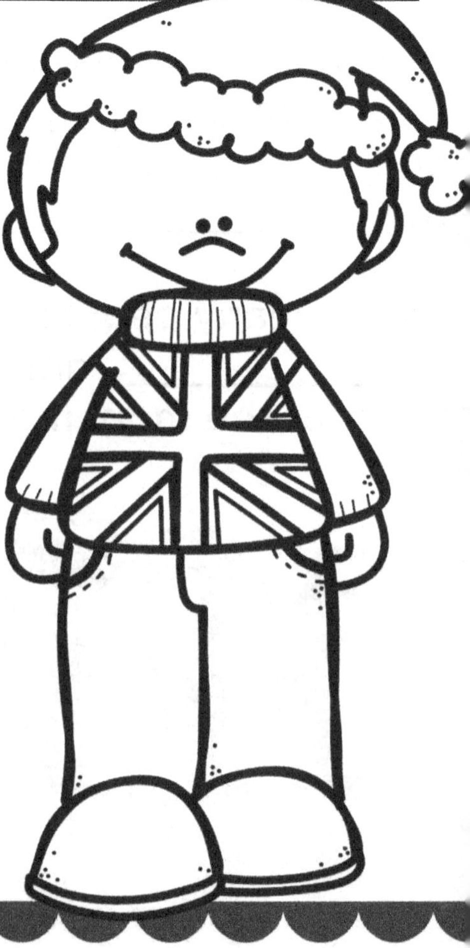

Answers:
1. That can't be better! 2. two weeks. 3. And that's that. 4. You are really smart. 5. I've gone crazy. 6. That's terrific. 7. You look great tonight. 8. She can't be trusted.

All About the USA

Color the American flag
red, white and blue

The United States of America is a country located in North America. Use an atlas to help you answer the questions. When you are done, color the map, and mark the capital with a star.

The capital of the USA is:

_____

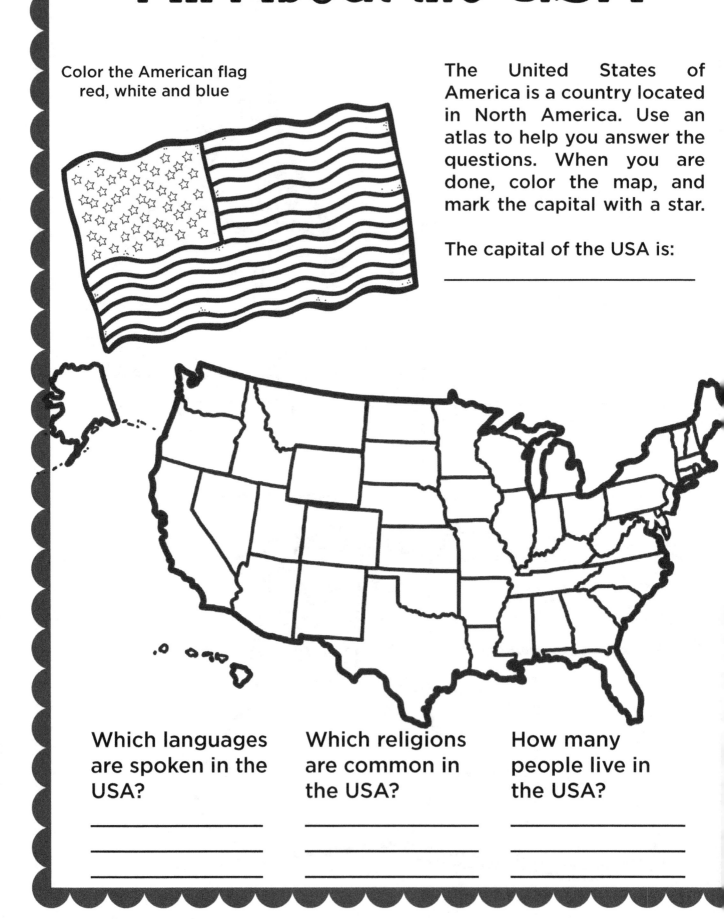

Which languages are spoken in the USA?

_____

_____

_____

Which religions are common in the USA?

_____

_____

_____

How many people live in the USA?

_____

_____

_____

Christmas at My House

My favorite Christmas tradition is:

_____
_____
_____
_____

Before Christmas my family always:

_____
_____
_____
_____

On Christmas Eve we:

_____
_____
_____

On Christmas Day we:

_____
_____
_____

For Christmas dinner, we like to eat:

_____
_____
_____
_____
_____

My family is special because:

_____
_____
_____

Gingerbread Houses

Use the word bank to fill in the blanks.

graham, Gretel, castle, Germany, Pastry, lucky,
holiday, White, women, Grimm, treats

Gingerbread houses originated in _____ during the 16th century. Gingerbread houses became very popular when the Brothers _____ wrote the story of Hansel and _____, in which the main characters stumble upon a house made entirely of _____ deep in the forest.

Today, many American families love to decorate gingerbread houses together during the _____ season! A gingerbread house does not have to be an actual house. It can be anything from a _____ to a small cabin, or another kind of building, such as a church, an art museum or a sports stadium. Other items, such as cars, gingerbread men and gingerbread _____, can be made of gingerbread dough. If you want to make a simple gingerbread house, you can make it out of _____ crackers. Anything goes!

One of the sweetest traditions at The _____ House is the unveiling of the official holiday gingerbread house. _____ chefs have created giant detailed gingerbread houses for the White House since the 1970's. Today, visitors can see the official gingerbread house if they are _____ enough to attend a tour during the holiday season.

Make A Popcorn Garland

Supplies:
Strong thread, such as nylon or waxed cotton; needle
1 cup popped popcorn per 3 to 4 feet of thread
3/4 cup cranberries per 3 to 4 feet of thread

Directions:
1. Place the popcorn in one bowl and the cranberries in another for easy access.
2. Thread the needle and make a large knot about 6 inches from the end of the thread.
3. Sew a garland of popcorn and cranberries, in any pattern you like. Place a knot after the last piece.
4. Hang the garland on your Christmas tree!

Unscramble the Christmas Words

1. ginJel slBle ☐☐☐☐☐ ☐☐☐☐☐

2. reMry tsmaCsrhi ☐☐☐☐☐ ☐☐☐☐☐☐☐☐☐

3. lteisn ☐☐☐☐☐☐

4. erpstsne ☐☐☐☐☐☐☐☐

5. nStaa sCalu ☐☐☐☐☐ ☐☐☐☐☐

6. tYduleie ☐☐☐☐☐☐☐☐

7. hlehBteme ☐☐☐☐☐☐☐☐☐

8. hpRdlou ☐☐☐☐☐☐☐

9. oeltmsite ☐☐☐☐☐☐☐☐☐

10. kfitucrae ☐☐☐☐☐☐☐☐☐

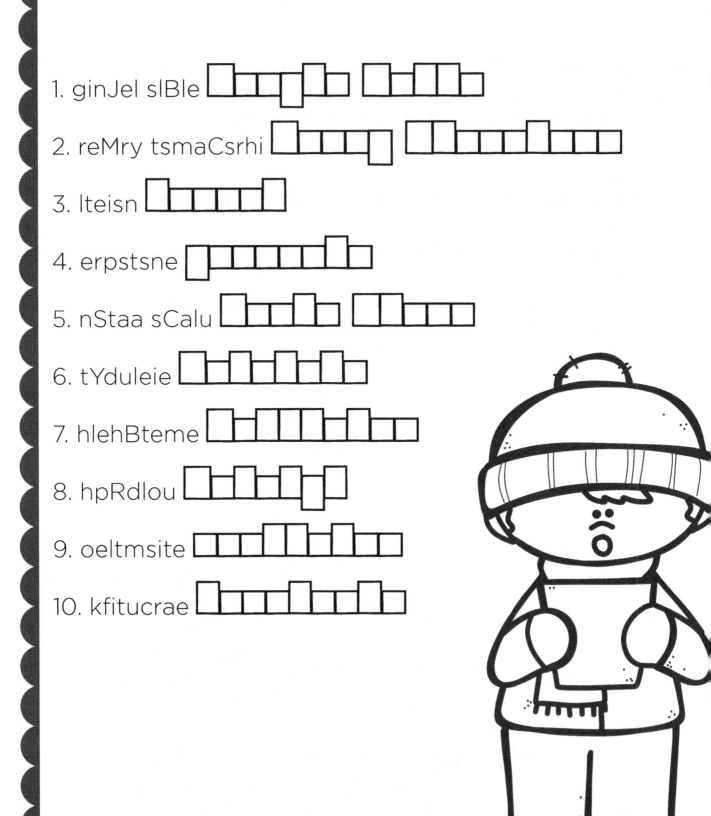

Kwanzaa

Kwanzaa is a holiday celebrated by many African-American families in the United States. The name 'Kwanzaa" comes from a Swahili phrase "matunda ya kwanza," which means "first fruits" and is celebrated from December 26th to January 1st. This seven-day celebration is dedicated to the "Nguzo Saba," which are the seven principles. Each night, families gather together to light a candle and discuss each of these principles.

Work with your family or use the Internet to define these principles.

unity/umoja:_____

_____

self-determination/kujichagulia:_____

_____

_____

collective responsibility/ujima:_____

_____

_____

cooperative economics/ujamaa:_____

_____

_____

purpose/nia:_____

_____

_____

creativity/kuumba:_____

_____

_____

faith/imani:_____

_____

Symbols of Kwanzaa

The Harvest

Kwanzaa is modeled after harvest festivals in Africa, which come after many months of hard work. People gather together as a community at the end of a long season to celebrate and share what they have grown together.

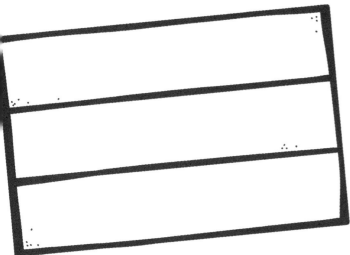

The Pan-African Flag

Red for blood - which unites all people of Black African ancestry, and has been shed for their freedom.
Black for people - who are a community, family and nation together.
Green for Africa - as a reminder of the beauty and wealth of Africa.

The Candles

The black candle is for Umoja (unity), which is known as the basis of success. It is lit first on December 26. The three green candles, representing Nia, Ujima, and Imani, are placed to the right of the Umoja candle, while the three red candles, representing Kujichagulia, Ujamaa, and Kuumba, are placed to the left of it. During Kwanzaa, one candle, representing one principle, is lit each day.

Kwanzaa was created for African-American families to enjoy a sense of community, to bring people together, and to celebrate their joint heritage. Describe the community your family is a part of: _____

_____
_____
_____
_____
_____

All About FRANCE

Color the French flag
red, white and blue

France is a country located in Europe. Use an atlas to help you answer the questions. When you are done, color the map, and mark the capital with a star.

The capital of France is:

_____

Which languages are spoken in France?

_____
_____
_____

Which religions are common in France?

_____
_____
_____

How many people live in France?

_____
_____
_____

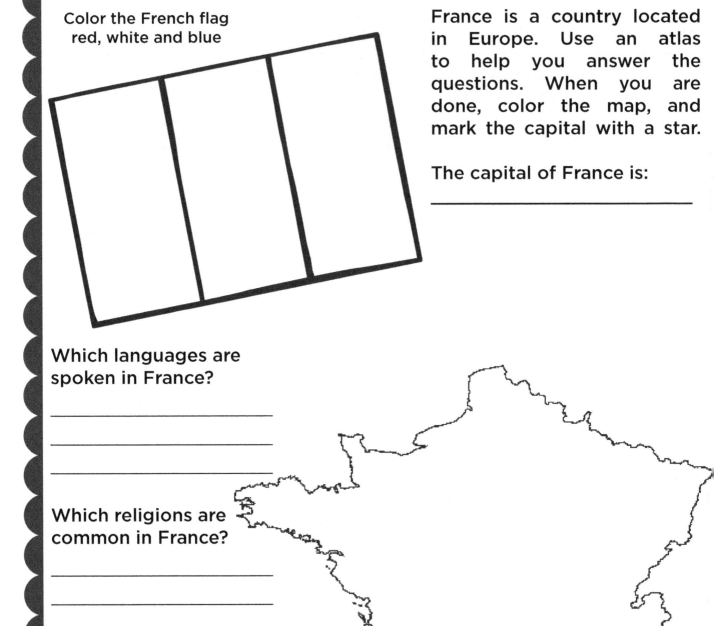

Christmas in France

Yule Logs made out of cherry wood are often burned in French homes at Christmas time. Families bring the log home on Christmas Eve. They sprinkle it with red wine to make the log smell really nice while it is burning. There is a custom that the log and candles are left burning all night with some food and drinks left out in case Mary and the baby Jesus come past during the night. The main Christmas meal, called Réveillon, is eaten on Christmas Eve in the middle of the night after families have returned from the midnight church service.

The meal typically includes roast turkey with chestnuts or roast goose, oysters, "foie gras," lobster, venison and cheeses.

For dessert, families often have a chocolate sponge cake log called a "bûche de Noël." In some parts of France, 13 different desserts are served for Christmas. All the desserts are made from different types of fruits and nuts.

Does your family eat a special Christmas meal? When do you eat it and what do you have?

_____
_____
_____
_____

The Church at Notre Dame

Use the word bank to fill in the blanks

bell, Paris, church, stained, Nativity, Advent, medieval, Notre, Roman, restored, gargoyles

In Paris, you'll find a giant stone _____ in the center of town. This church is called _____ Dame, and is one of the most famous churches in the whole world. It is a _____ catholic church, and it took over 200 years to build! It was finally completed in the year 1345.

Notre Dame Cathedral is still in use today by the _____ Catholic Church for Sunday mass, and many people visit it every day to see the artwork and _____ glass windows inside.

Notre Dame also has a famous _____ but there is no bell ringer. The church has been modernized so it now rings automatically. Visitors can climb the 140-step staircase to see the historical bell, visit the _____, or have a glimpse of the city of _____!

Many people don't know that the gargoyles are "new" and were added to the church in the late 1800's when the church was _____.

Notre Dame is decorated each Christmas season with a giant Christmas tree outside. Inside, you'll find _____ scenes, the star of Bethlehem and an _____ wreath.

Make Galette des Rois

Ingredients:

1/4 cup almond paste
1/4 cup white sugar
3 tablespoons butter, softened
1 egg
1/4 teaspoon vanilla extract
1/4 teaspoon almond extract

2 tablespoons all-purpose flour
1 pinch salt
1 package frozen puff pastry, thawed
1 dry kidney bean
1 egg, beaten
1 tablespoon confectioners' sugar for dusting

Directions:

1. Place the almond paste into a food processor or blender with about half of the sugar, and mix until well blended.
2. Add the butter and remaining sugar, egg, vanilla, almond extract, flour and salt. Set aside.
3. Preheat the oven to 425 degrees. Grease a baking sheet.
4. Roll out one sheet of the puff pastry into an 11-inch square. Use a large plate to trace an 11 inch circle onto the dough using the tip of a small knife. Place the circle of pastry onto the prepared baking sheet. Repeat with the second sheet of pastry. Refrigerate both sheets.
5. Mound the almond filling onto the center of the pastry that is on the baking sheet. Leave about 1 1/2-inch margin at the edges. Press the bean down into the filling.
6. Place the second sheet of pastry on top, and press down the edges to seal. Beat the remaining egg with a fork, and lightly brush onto the top of the galette. Use a knife to make a crisscross pattern in the egg wash, and then prick several small slits in the top to vent steam while baking.
7. Bake for 15 minutes in the preheated oven. Remove from the oven, and dust with confectioners' sugar. Return to the oven, and cook for an additional 12 to 15 minutes, or until the top is a deep golden brown. Transfer to a wire rack to cool.
8. Lay a golden paper crown gently on top of the cake. This will be used to crown the person who finds the bean. Serve warm or cold. Make sure to tell everyone about the bean!

Fun with the French Language

Can you and your family figure out the translation of these French words?

1. Joyeux Noël ☐☐☐☐☐ ☐☐☐☐☐☐☐☐☐

2. La crèche ☐☐☐☐☐☐☐

3. Un cadeau ☐☐☐☐

4. Un sucre d'orge ☐☐☐☐☐ ☐☐☐☐

5. Une étoile ☐☐☐☐

1.Merry Christmas, 2. manger, 3. gift, 4. candy cane, 5. star

Word Search Word List:
Joyeux Noël, Merry Christmas, La crèche,
Manger, France, Un cadeau, Gift, Un sucre d'orge,
Candy Cane, Une étoile, Star

I	S	P	G	H	R	V	D	N	U	F	C	R	N	O
O	N	A	I	U	A	E	D	A	C	P	X	Y	W	Y
C	L	O	M	L	E	O	N	X	U	E	Y	O	J	T
L	K	I	V	T	F	E	T	O	I	L	E	W	K	F
P	U	Z	S	I	S	R	E	O	N	T	I	G	U	I
C	U	D	U	H	N	I	A	D	U	F	W	X	D	G
P	B	D	C	L	Z	O	R	N	R	O	H	L	V	P
C	N	Y	R	Y	G	T	O	H	C	Q	O	E	B	N
A	B	Y	E	M	Z	P	G	C	C	E	K	X	Z	N
C	V	B	D	K	S	I	A	E	M	Y	U	Z	A	N
R	D	H	O	R	N	N	Y	F	U	A	R	E	J	U
E	W	O	R	O	E	D	R	A	T	S	N	R	O	B
C	F	X	G	H	N	F	M	X	M	X	E	G	E	P
H	Q	O	E	A	V	W	G	W	M	F	R	T	E	M
E	U	R	C	D	Y	Z	E	T	O	F	U	V	G	R

All About ISRAEL

Color the Israeli flag blue and white.

Israel is a country located in the Middle East. Use an atlas to help you answer the questions. When you are done, color the map, and mark the capital with a star.

The capital of Israel is:

_____

Which languages are spoken in Israel?

_____
_____
_____

Which religions are common in Israel?

_____
_____
_____

How many people live in Israel?

_____
_____
_____

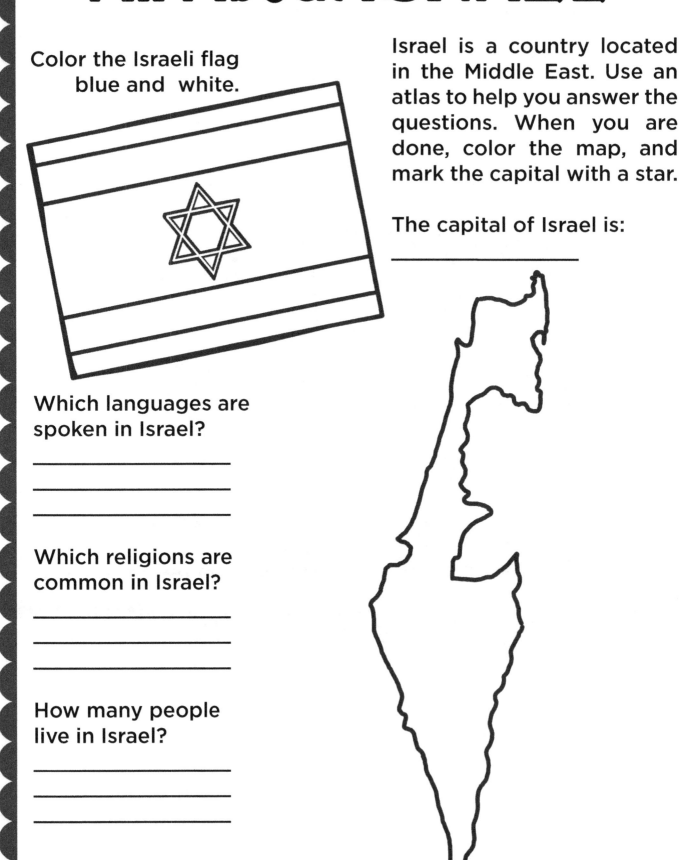

Hanukkah

The Festival of Lights

Hanukkah is a Jewish holiday that celebrates two miracles that happened long ago in a country called Judea (now known as Israel). Back then the Jewish people who lived in Judea were under the rule of an evil king who refused to let them practice their religion. The evil king even destroyed their holy temple in Jerusalem by covering it with graffiti, and letting animals live inside it, which destroyed all the sacred oil the Jews had prepared.

A group of young men known as Maccabees decided to fight the evil king in order to have the freedom to follow any religion they chose. The first miracle was that even though there were very few Maccabees, they were able to win and kick the evil king's soldiers out of Jerusalem.

The second miracle happened when they went back into their holy temple. The Jewish people wanted to light the menorah, which is the holy candelabra, but they only found enough sacred oil to burn for one day. Back then, it took eight days to make more oil. They decided to light the menorah anyway, and somehow the oil lasted for eight days instead of just one.

The word Hanukkah means "rededication," because it celebrates the Jewish people rededicating their holy temple and the miracles that helped make it happen.

How would you feel if you had to hide your religion or some other important part of who you are?

_____

_____

_____

_____

Dreidel Dreidel

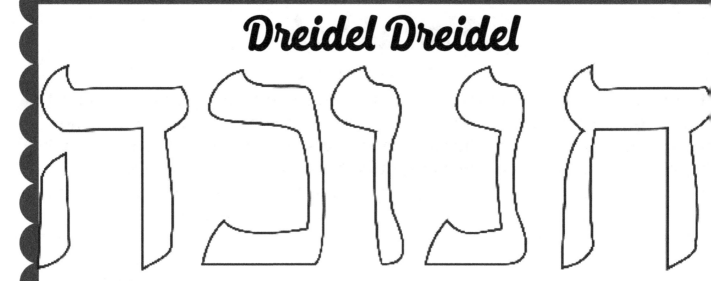

Back in the time of the Maccabees, Jews had to pray and practice their religion in secret. If the evil king's soldiers came around, the Jews needed a reason to be gathered, so they would hide their prayer books and take out spinning tops. These spinning tops are called dreidels. The dreidel game is still played by Jewish children during the celebration of Hanukkah.

The four symbols on the sides of the dreidel are Hebrew letters. The letters are an acronym: Nun, Gimmel, Hay, and Shin, for the sentence (transliterated from Hebrew) Nes Gadol Haya Sham. The sentence means "A Great Miracle Happened There."

Fun Fact: Dreidels in Israel have the letter Pay instead of Shin, because there the sentence means "A Great Miracle Happened Here," since the story of Hanukkah took place in what is now Israel.

In order to play, you need some pennies, raisins, M&Ms or something similar. Each player gets an equal amount of the pennies. The first player spins the dreidel. Depending on which side the dreidel lands on, one of four things happens:

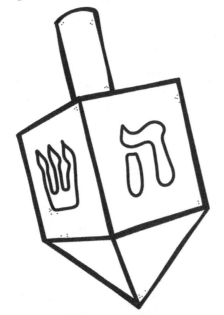

Nun = Nothing (The player doesn't get any pennies from the pot)

Gimmel = You Win (The player receives the entire pot of pennies)

Hey = Half (The player receives half of the pot of pennies)

Shin = Put One In (The player has to place one of their own pennies into the pot)

Make Latkes

Latkes are a traditional Hanukkah food. They are cooked in oil, and the story says that the Maccabees came through town on their way to battle, and the families in the village were able to quickly mix up a batch for the soldiers to eat. The food helped make them strong, and they won the battle!

Ingredients:
  2 potatoes
  1/2 an onion
  2 tablespoons flour
  2 eggs
  1/2 teaspoon salt
  1/4 teaspoon pepper
  Oil for frying

Directions:
  1. Clean the potatoes. Grate them into a large bowl.
  2. Peel the onion. Grate it into the same bowl.
  3. Add the flour, eggs, salt and pepper. Mix it all up!
  4. Heat the oil in a frying pan.
  5. Drop the potato mixture into the pan using a tablespoon scoop.
  6. Flatten each latke with a spoon while it cooks.
  7. Turn the latkes in the pan, browning each side.
  8. Remove from the pan and let them cool on a paper towel.
  9. Serve warm with a dollop of apple sauce.

* Kids, hot oil is very dangerous. Cook latkes with Mom or Dad's help!*

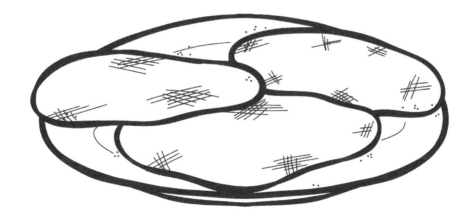

The Menorah

Families light the menorah right after sunset on each of the eight Hanukkah nights, except for on Friday night, when the candle is lit before sunset. Many families keep the menorah in the window to spread the Hanukkah light, so others can see it and remember God's miracles.

Before the candles are lit, families say a special prayer. On the first night, they recite three blessings in Hebrew. On the other nights, they recite two blessings.

A special candle, called the Shamesh candle is used to light the Hanukkah candles. It is placed higher than the other eight candles. The candles are then lit from the left to the right, with one candle lit the first night, two on the second, and so on.

Color the menorah:
Color the Shamesh candle a different color than the others, and color the remaining candles from left to right.

Hanukkah Words

Dreidel – A spinning top used by ancient Jews to hide their religious practice and now used by children to play a fun game.

Hannukiyah – Also known as a menorah, a Hannukiyah is a candelabra that has eight branches and an additional holder for a ninth candle. One candle is added for each night of Hanukkah and the additional candle helps light the others.

Latke – A potato pancake fried in oil. Latkes are a traditional food eaten on Hanukkah, because they are fried in oil (just like the sacred oil from the holy temple).

Suffganiyah – Jelly donuts are another traditional Hanukkah food since they are fried in oil.

Gelt – Commonly refers to chocolate money (though it could mean real money too).

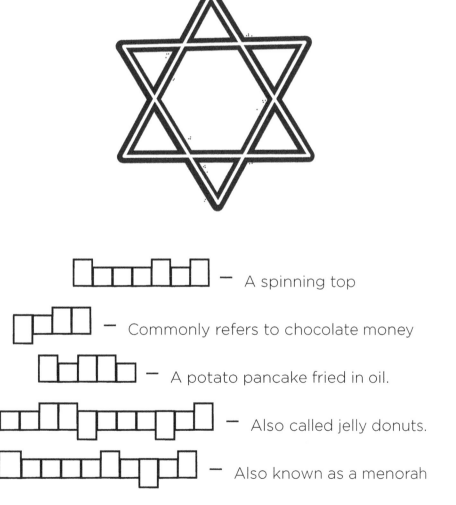

— A spinning top

— Commonly refers to chocolate money

— A potato pancake fried in oil.

— Also called jelly donuts.

— Also known as a menorah

Made in the USA
Las Vegas, NV
06 November 2020